Francis Fowke

Extracts from the Records at the East India House

Of Proceedings Relative to Mr. Francis Fowke, Resident of Benares

Francis Fowke

Extracts from the Records at the East India House
Of Proceedings Relative to Mr. Francis Fowke, Resident of Benares

ISBN/EAN: 9783337059231

Printed in Europe, USA, Canada, Australia, Japan

Cover: Foto ©Suzi / pixelio.de

More available books at **www.hansebooks.com**

EXTRACTS

FROM THE

RECORDS

AT THE

EAST INDIA HOUSE,

OF

PROCEEDINGS

RELATIVE TO

MR. FRANCIS FOWKE,

RESIDENT OF BENARES.

IN THE APPOINTMENT AND RE-APPOINTMENT OF HIM
TO THAT RESIDENCY, AND HIS FIRST AND SECOND
RECALL FROM THENCE.

.

LIST of PAPERS.

No. I. EXTRACT of the proceedings of the Governor General and Council in their Secret Department, Fort William, the 16th Auguſt 1775. Preſent, the Governor General, General Clavering, Colonel Monſon, Mr. Barwell, and Mr. Francis. *Firſt appointment of Mr. Francis Fowke to Benares.*

No. II. Copy of the 10th paragraph of a Letter from the Governor General and Council in Bengal, in their Secret Department, to the Court of Directors of the Eaſt India Companv, dated 11th September 1775. *Notification of the appointment of Mr. Francis Fowke to Benares.*

No. III. Extract of Bengal Secret Conſultations, the 2d December 1776. Preſent, the Governor General, General Clavering, Mr. Barwell, and Mr. Francis. *Recall of Mr. Francis Fowke from Benares.*

No. IV. Extract of a Letter from General Clavering to the Court of Directors, dated 5th December 1776. *On the removal of Mr. Briſtow from Oude, and Mr. Francis Fowke from Benares.*

No. V. Copy of the 6th paragraph of the General Letter from Bengal, (ſecret department,) dated 22d December 1776. *Notification of the Recall of Mr. Francis Fowke from Benares.*

A 2

No,

No.

cent. on his expenditures, and permiſſion to draw for his preſent ſalary of 1000 *Rupees per month to the time he enters on the Agency and three months after.*

N. B. As the records of Council for January 1781, have not yet been received by the Court of Directors, the Extract No. XXVII. has been furniſhed by favour of Major John Scott, Agent for the Governor General in political Concerns.

*Extract of the Proceedings of the Governor General and
Council, in their Secret Department, Fort William, the
16th August, 1775. Present, the Governor General,
General Clavering, Colonel Monson, Mr. Barwell, and
Mr. Francis.*

GENERAL Clavering moves, that a Company's
servant be sent up to Benares, to carry with him
the *Sunnuds* of investiture to the Raja from the Company, and to inform himself of the nature of the mint,
the species of rupees that are coined in it, how much the
person who farmed it paid to the Soubah of Oude, or to
his ministers, in presents; as likewise with the nature of
the cutwally, and what the advantages of it were to the
person who farmed it; in order to make such a settlement
with the Raja as may be equally advantageous to him
and the Company.

Mr. Francis agrees to the motion.

Mr. Barwell. I looked upon the motion to be carried
by the last resolution of the board, and that the choice
of a person remains only to be determined. The Company, in the extra charges to which they have already
been put, may have occasion to complain; and as œco-
nomy and dispatch may be equally promoted, I beg leave
to mention Colonel Main, the officer commanding at
Chunar, as the most eligible person: little or no charges
will be incurred by his just moving from Chunar to
Benares; and, besides, he is the best qualified, from his
local knowledge.

B   Colonel

Colonel Monſon agrees to the motion of General Clavering.

The Governor General objects to this motion.

Reſolved, a covenanted ſervant be appointed to go to Benares, to take the *Sunnuds* of inveſtiture to the Rajah, &c. alſo to make the inveſtigations neceſſary to enable the board to come to a final ſettlement with the Rajah for that Zemindary.

General Clavering moves, that Mr. Francis Fowke be appointed to execute this ſervice; a young man exceedingly well qualified, from his knowledge in the Perſian tongue, and his unexceptionable good character.

Mr. Francis. I believe Mr. Francis Fowke to be perfectly qualified for the ſervice propoſed; and I agree to the motion.

Mr. Barwell. The unhappy differences that have prevailed at the board, the particular part which Mr. Joſeph Fowke has acted ſince the commencement of the new government, the particular predicament in which he ſtands at preſent, I am ſorry to obſerve, makes Mr. Francis Fowke, his ſon, the moſt improper nomination for a commiſſion of this kind that could have been thought of; nor can I conceive why it ſhould have been thought of, unleſs for the expreſs purpoſe of lowering the Governor General in the eyes of the Raja of Benares, as well as of all India, by the ſelection of this gentleman. I have no other objection to Mr. Francis Fowke. Was it in my power I would ſerve him, but not at the expence, or in degradation of the firſt character of the ſtate. I therefore wiſh that Mr. Francis Fowke's nomination may not be carried.

Colonel Monſon. I do not comprehend Mr. Barwell's chain of reaſoning, that the employing an unexceptionable Company's ſervant can be any degradation to the Governor General's conſequence or honour, or lower his dignity in the eyes of the public: had Mr. Francis Fowke been an exceptionable character, there might have been ſome degree of juſtneſs in Mr. Barwell's obſervation; but, as Mr. Barwell himſelf declares he wiſhes to ſerve him, I do not comprehend why
he

he will not on this occafion teftify to Mr. Fowke this in-
clination. I believe Mr. Fowke to be qualified for this
appointment, and therefore approve of the nomination.

General Clavering is for his own nomination.

The Governor General. I am not furprized at the
motion now before the board : I expected it at the time
in which it was refolved, in contradiction to the former
opinion of the board, to permit Mr. Jofeph Fowke to return to Benares. I confider the prefent appointment as
the appointment, not of Mr. Francis Fowke, but of Mr.
Jofeph Fowke, whofe influence over his fon will reduce
the authority of the latter to a mere fhadow ; I therefore
difapprove of the motion ; I proteft againft it.

Agreed, that Mr. Francis Fowke be appointed to proceed to Benares, for the purpofes already refolved on.

Ordered, that inftructions be prepared for him accordingly, with a letter of credence to Raja Cheyt Sing.

No. II.

*Extract of a Letter from the Governor General and Council
in Bengal, in their Secret Department, to the Court of
Directors of the Eaft India Company, dated 11th September, 1775.*

Par. 10. IN our Letter of the 3d Auguft, of which
you will receive a duplicate by this fhip, you
are advifed of the acquifition of the territories of Raja
Cheyt Sing to the Company, and of the fteps which we
had then taken towards fettling with him for that Zemindary. On the 16th of that month we again took this
fubject into confideration, and called the Vakeel before
us, who had received an anfwer from his mafter to our
firft offer ; but not being able to afcertain from him the
finenefs and quantity of the filver of the Gourfhay Rupees, in which coin the tribute from the Rajah is to be
paid, nor the exact amount which the late Farmers of the
Mint and Cutwally at Benares, and the Cutwally at Juan-

pore, had paid annually to the Nabob and his Officers for the grant of those articles, we judged it neceffary to appoint a perfon to proceed to Benares, to make fundry local inveftigations into thefe and other points, to enable us to come to a final adjuftment with the Raja; and we accordingly appointed Mr. Francis Fowke. In the mean time, we agreed that the Raja fhould continue to pay at Benares the exact fum, and in the fame fpecies of ru-pees, as he had paid to the late and prefent Nabobs of Oude, that is to fay, 23,72,65612 Gourfhay rupees, ex-clufive of the Mint, Cutwally, and other articles, which the Nabob held in his own right.

No. III.

Extract of Bengal Secret Confultations, the 2d December, 1776. Prefent, the Governor General, General Cla-vering, Mr. Barwell, and Mr. Francis.

THE Governor General alfo moves, that Mr. Francis Fowke be recalled from Benares, and his com-miffion annulled; the exprefs purpofes thereof having been accomplifhed.

Mr. Francis. I need not bring my opinion in writing upon either of thefe motions. To the firft I make no objection; but as to the recal of Mr. Francis Fowke, I know no motive for it; on the contrary, I am fatisfied that his prefence at Benares has been of fignal ufe in preventing the delays of the remittance of the tribute; and to my knowledge he has done nothing to incur the difpleafure of the board; I cannot therefore confent to his recal.

Mr. Barwell. The exprefs purpofes to which Mr. Fowke was firft appointed, were, the inveftiture of the Raja, and the fettling a mode for the remittance of his tribute: his commiffion ceafed the inftant the object of it

was

was accomplifhed, and Mr. Fowke ought then to have been remanded to Calcutta; he holds no appointment, and therefore it cannot properly be ftyled a removal. I affent therefore to Mr. Fowke's being called to the prefidency.

General Clavering. In regard to the recal of Mr. Fowke, and the annulling of his office, I cannot help confidering it as a vindictive meafure, couched under the appearance of public fervice, and therefore diffent to the motion.

Governor General. I agree to the motion.

Refolved, that the motion propofed by the Governor General be carried in the affirmative.

The following letter is accordingly written to Mr. Fowke.

To Mr. Francis Fowke.

Sir,

The objects propofed by your appointment, to proceed to Benares, being now accomplifhed, we have thought it neceffary to annul the commiffion which was given you for that purpofe: We therefore direct that you return to this prefidency immediately on receipt hereof.

We are, &c.

No. IV.

Extract of a Letter from General Clavering to the Court of Directors, dated 5th December, 1776.

THE reftraint that I had laid on myfelf not to infringe further on the rules of the fervice than was neceffary, for the explanation of my conduct in the part I am obliged to take, gives way again to the obligation I feel myfelf under, in the ftrict difcharge of my duty, to acquaint you with fome of the laft tranfactions of the council after the departure of the Naffau, as their being undertaken precifely at that juncture feems calculated to conceal, as long as poffible, the information of them from your notice.

The

The firft fubject is, the removal of Mr. Briftow from
the poft of Refident with the Vizier, and the re-appointment of Mr. Middleton. The next is, the recal of
Mr. Francis Fowke from Benares.

Having annexed the entire confultation on both fub-
jects, I will forbear to make any reflections on the proceedings, leaving it to your honourable board to decide,
how far the good of your fervice has been confulted in
removing two gentlemen, who have each diftinguifhed
themfelves; the firft, in obtaining for the Company an
addition of thirty lacks a year to their former revenue ;
and the fecond, in re-eftablifhing the coinage of Benares,
by means of which the exact amount of the fubfidy is
afcertained, and then fixing the rate of the remittance on
the moft advantageous terms to the Company. As to
Mr. Middleton's re-appointment, you yourfelves, gentlemen, as well as the proprietors, are too much in-
terefted in the fupport of your own dignity, and too
fenfibly wounded in the ftep taken to reftore him to an
office from which he had been difmiffed, after the fo-
lemn condemnation which you had given on his conduct
for not fubmitting his correfpondence to the fupreme
council, for me to mention and lay a ftrefs on the little
regard the chief of a council fhews to the honour of a
government over which he prefides, to recommend a fervant to fill any poft till he has made the fatisfaction required of him, not only to the government in which he
ferves, but to his mafters and fuperiors, on whom he ul-
timately depends.

No. V.

*Extract of the Secret General Letter from Bengal, dated
22d December, 1776.*

Par. 6. THE purpofes for which Mr. Francis Fowke
was appointed to proceed to Raja Cheyt
Sing, at Benares, being now fully accomplifhed, we have
annulled his commiffion, and ordered him to return to
the prefidency.

No.

No. VI.

Extract of Bengal Secret Consultations, the 23d December, 1776. Present, the Governor General, General Clavering, Mr. Barwell, and Mr. Francis.

THE Governor General moves, that a civil servant of the Company be appointed to reside at Benares on the part of this government, for the purpose of transacting any occasional business which may arise between this government and the Raja of Benares; and that Mr. Thomas Graham may be nominated to this office, and Mr. Daniel Barwell to be his assistant.

Mr. Francis. If a civil servant was necessary for the purpose described in the motion, I conceive that Mr. Francis Fowke was perfectly well qualified for that office. I have no objection, however, to either of the gentlemen recommended by the Governor General.

Mr. Barwell agrees to the motion.

General Clavering. I object to it, and leave the responsibility of the measure with the Governor General, who must answer for it.

Resolved, that a civil servant of the Company be appointed to reside at Benares, on the part of this government, for the purpose of transacting any occasional business which may arise between this government and the Raja of Benares.

Agreed, that Mr. Thomas Graham be nominated to this office; and that Mr. Daniel Barwell be appointed his assistant.

No. VII.

Extract of the Secret General Letter from Bengal, dated 6th January, 1777.

Par. 11. WE have thought it proper to appoint a Company's servant to reside at Benares, for the purpose of transacting any occasional business that may arise between this government and Raja Cheyt Sing. This appointment has been given to Mr. Thomas Graham, and Mr. D. O. Barwell has been nominated his assistant.

No.

No. VIII.

Extract of the Company's General Letter to Bengal, dated 30th January, 1778.

Par. 65. IN your fecret letter of the 19th of December, 1776, you inform us, that the purpofes for which Mr. Francis Fowke was appointed to proceed to Benares being fully accomplifhed, you had annulled his commiffion, and ordered him to the prefidency; but it appears by your letter of the 6th of January, 1777, that in lefs than twenty days you thought proper to appoint Mr. Thomas Graham to refide at Benares, and Mr. Daniel Octavus Barwell to be his affiftant.

Par. 66. If it were poffible to fuppofe that a faving to the Company had been your motive for annulling Mr. Fowke's commiffion, we fhould have approved your proceedings; but when we find two perfons appointed immediately afterwards, with two falaries, to execute an office which had been filled with reputation by Mr. Fowke alone, and that Mr. Graham enjoys all the emoluments annexed to the office of Mr. Fowke, we muft be of opinion, that Mr. Fowke was removed without juft caufe, to make room for Mr. Graham; and that the addition of Mr. Barwell's falary is a clear lofs of three hundred rupees per month to the Company.

Par. 67. As it was not pretended that Mr. Fowke's conduct had been exceptionable, as he had executed with the greateft punctuality and exactnefs the like office to which you have now appointed Mr. Graham; and as the diffent of Mr. Francis, and the proteft of General Clavering, on the occafion, had no effect, we think it proper to interfere; and therefore direct, that Mr. Francis Fowke be immediately reinftated in his office of Refident and Poft-mafter at Benares; we however think proper to declare, that though we mean by this order to do an act of public juftice, we by no means intend it as a mark of difapprobation of the conduct of Mr. Graham, whom we believe to be a very deferving fervant of the Company.

No.

Extract of Bengal Public Consultations, the 20th July, 1778. Present, the Governor General, and Messrs. Barwell, Francis, and Wheler.

READ the general letter, dated 30th January last, received from the Hon. the Court of Directors by the Grosvenor and Osterly.

Par. 65, 66, and 67. Governor General. I must request that the board will suspend the execution of this order. The spirit and intention of it is evident, and publicly known both in England and here. With these considerations in view, my consent to the recal of Mr. Graham would be adequate to my own resignation of the service, because it would inflict such a wound in my authority and influence, that I could not maintain it. In the course of a few days we may expect to hear of the resolutions which have been taken by our superiors, and of the appointments which have been made to fill the vacancy occasioned in this government, by the death of the late Sir John Clavering. These will be likewise decisive of my own situation in the service. I need not say more to urge the propriety of suspending the execution of this order of the Court of Directors. Mr. Thompson, in his letter from Marseilles, dated the 18th of April, mentions that a packet, containing the news of the General's death, had been dispatched to London from that port, from his Majesty's agent there, seven days before, and it is probable that the Swallow carried this intelligence earlier. We may therefore expect, that the Caranja, which was to depart from Suez immediately on receipt of the confirmation of the war, will bring us those decisive orders which I look for; and these may arrive to-morrow, or in the course of a very few days.

Mr. Francis. The Court of Directors order Mr. Francis Fowke to be *immediately* reinstated in his office.

C   To

To fufpend the execution of fuch an order is to difobey it. In another part of the fame letter (par. 41) they fay, " We can on no account permit our orders to be " difobeyed, and our authority difregarded." When the Company's orders to me are clear and pofitive, I do not deem myfelf at liberty to with-hold my obedience to them on any confideration whatever; unlefs a new fi-tuation of affairs unknown to, and unforefeen by, the Court of Directors, fhould make it impracticable or dan-gerous to carry them into execution: I am therefore againft the motion.

Mr. Wheler. I am of opinion that the order fhould be immediately carried into execution.

Mr. Barwell. While Mr. Haftings is in the govern-ment, the refpect and dignity of his ftation fhould be fupported. In thefe fentiments I muft decline an ac-quiefcence in any order which has a tendency to bring the government into difrepute; as the Company have the means and the power of forming their own admi-niftration in India, they may at their pleafure place whom they pleafe at the head. But, in my opinion, they are uot authorized to treat a perfon in that poft with indignity.

Refolved, that the execution of this order be fuf-pended.

Mr. Francis. I beg leave to enter my diffent to this refolution.

No. X.

Copy of a Letter from Mr. Francis Fowke to the Secretary of the Superior Council in Bengal.

To J. P. Auriol, Efq; Secretary to the Hon. the Su-perior Council.

Sir,   Calcutta, 21ft July, 1778.

MY friends in England having tranfmitted to me a notification in form, which they have received, importing, that an order of the Honourable the Court of Directors, for my inftant re-appointment to the poft
of

of Refident at Benares, was tranfmitted by the Grofvenor, and a confiderable time being now elapfed fince the receipt of the packet, I humbly requeft of the Honourable Board, that I may be informed of any refolutions which may have paffed in confequence of the above order, and that I may be furnifhed with a copy of their proceedings upon the fubjeft.

I am, Sir,
Your obedient humble fervant,
FRANCIS FOWKE.

No. XI.

Copy of a Letter from the Secretary of the Superior Council, in Bengal, to Mr. Francis Fowke.

To Mr. Francis Fowke.

Sir,

IN confequence of your addrefs to the Hon. the Governor General and Council, requefting to be informed of any refolutions which may have paffed on the orders of the Court of Direftors refpefting you, and to be furnifhed with a copy of the proceedings upon the fubjeft, I am direfted to tranfmit you the enclofed extraft of the confultation, 20th inftant.

Council Chamber,
the 29th July, 1778.

I am, Sir,
Your moft obedient fervant,
J. P. AURIOL.

Extraft of Confultation, 20th July, 1778.

Read the General Letter, dated the 30th January laft, received from the Hon. the Court of Direftors, by the Grofvenor and Ofterly.

Par. 64, 65, 66, and 67. Refolved, that the execution of this order be fufpended.

A true extraft.
J. P. AURIOL, Secretary.

Copy of a Letter from Mr. Francis Fowke to the Governor General and Council in Bengal.

To the Hon, Warren Haftings, Efq; Governor General, &c. Superior Council of Fort William.

Hon. Sirs,

I Acknowledge with great thankfulnefs your condefcenfion, in conveying to me, through Mr. Secretary Auriol, the refolution you have paffed to fufpend the execution of the Company's order, dated 30th January, 1778, directing, that "Mr. Francis Fowke be immediately reinftated in his office of Refident and poftmafter at Benares." By this indulgence I have an opportunity afforded me of humbly remonftrating againft the feverity of your fentence, which is nearly equal to difmiffion from the fervice.

An order of the Court of Directors, made public only a few days ago, pofitively forbids any covenanted fervant to return to England, under any pretence of obtaining redrefs there for injuries received here, without firft making an appeal to them through the channel of the Prefident and Council abroad. The exiftence of this order neceffarily fuppofes that no covenanted fervant can be difmiffed or fufpended from his offices in India without fome previous trial, at leaft fome charge or fome accufation to which he may be fuffered to reply. On any other fuppofition the Court of Directors can have no materials lying before them to conduct their judgment of his merits. I ftand exactly in this predicament, and fubmit to your candour to determine whether the cafe be not a hard one. I fee a fimple refolution which fufpends me from my offices, and am left to guefs at the caufes which influence it. In fuch a fituation I cannot be free from anxiety. Confcious of my own innocence

nocence and integrity, I *will* hope that your juſtice will relieve me. If there are any accuſations laid againſt me, let my accuſers ſtand forth ; let me anſwer them face to face : I muſt believe there are ſome, becauſe I am confident your juſtice would not permit me to be condemned on *no* grounds, however you might have miſtaken them.

I am ſenſible that my ſituation obliges me to the moſt perfect ſubmiſſion to your orders; yet, as my own honour, and that of my family, will not allow me to ſit ſilent under a diſgrace, it was a duty incumbent upon me to defend my reputation. In the offices I have filled, I have ſtrictly adhered to my duty, and cannot charge myſelf with having ever been deficient in reſpect to my ſuperiors. The ſame conduct I ſhall ever obſerve. If you find, on a candid examination, that the merit I lay claim to is my due, I truſt that your Hon. Board will be pleaſed to carry into execution the Hon. the Court of Directors orders, for my immediate reappointment to the offices of preſident and poſtmaſter at Benares.

I remain, with the greateſt reſpect,
Honourable Sir and Sirs,
Your moſt faithful
and moſt obedient ſervant,
FRANCIS FOWKE.

Calcutta,
12th Auguſt, 1778.

No. XIII.

Extract of the General Letter from Bengal, dated 17th Auguſt, 1778.

Par. 25. WE have reſolved to ſuſpend the execution of that part of your commands, dated 30th January laſt, which relate to Mr. Francis Fowke, and muſt beg leave to refer you to our records for the motives which ſwayed with us in this inſtance.

No. XIV.

*Extract of Bengal Public Consultations, the 7th September,
1778. Present, the Governor General, and Messrs.
Barwell, Francis, and Wheler.*

READ a letter from Mr. Fowke. See No. XII.
Mr. Francis. I move, that the Secretary may be
directed to inform Mr. Francis Fowke, that the board
have no reason to be dissatisfied with any part of his conduct in the Company's Service, and that no charge has
been preferred against him to the board.

Mr. Wheler. I agree to the motion.

Mr. Barwell. The board having already denied to
Mr. Fowke the satisfaction he required, by ordering
simply the resolution of the board to be furnished by the
Secretary, I move the previous question.

Mr. Wheler and Mr. Francis against the motion.

Governor General. I am for the previous question.
All applications of this kind are irregular. The board
are not accountable to Mr. Fowke for their resolution
respecting him. The reasons for suspending the execution of the orders of the Court of Directors contain no
charge, nor the slightest imputation of a charge, against
Mr. Fowke; but I see no reason why the board should
condescend to tell him so.

The previous question being carried,

Resolved, that Mr. Francis's question be not put.

No. XV.

*Extract of Bengal Public Consultations, the 1st April,
1779. Present, the Governor General, Messrs. Barwell,
Francis, and Wheler, and Sir Eyre Coote.*

MR. Francis. I move, that the 65th, 66th, and
67th paragraphs of the Company's general letter
of the 30th January, 1778, and the proceedings of this
board of the 20th July, 1778, be now read.

Read

Read the paragraphs 65, 66, and 67 of the general letter, dated the 30th January, 1778, and the proceedings of the 20th July, 1778.

Mr. Francis. I move, that the Company's orders, contained in the preceding paragraphs, be carried into execution; that Mr. Francis Fowke be immediately reinftated in his office of Refident and Poft-mafter at Benares; and that Mr. Thomas Graham be ordered to deliver over charge of thofe offices forthwith to Mr. Francis Fowke.

Governor General. I have expected this motion, and I expect many more of a fimilar nature to be introduced by Mr. Francis, for the purpofe of forcing the new member of this government to declare himfelf a party in difputes in which he has no concern, and in which I will venture to exprefs my belief that it is not his wifh to be involved. The order of the Company which has been read was addreffed to this adminiftration before Sir Eyre Coote was a member of it. It was alfo read, and a refolution paffed upon it, before Sir Eyre Coote's appointment. I prefume, therefore, to fay, that it is irregularly brought before the board at this time. For though his voice may be now required, and may be given upon the motion, yet, as it refpects the act of a former adminiftration, and an act already done, the refponfibility of that act refts only with thofe who conftitutionally paffed it, and ought not to be thrown upon him, unlefs he is defirous that it fhould be revifed, and that he may participate in it. If our records are to undergo a new fcrutiny, and every meafure which they contain to be examined by the fcale of the Company's orders, or by the judgment of the prefent adminiftration, the time of the board will not fuffice, even in a daily meeting of it, for fo multiplied a refearch, and for the debates which muft neceffarily accompany it. If this retrofpect is not to affect all the refolutions and all the meafures of the paffed government, on what principle is a felection made of a queftion which has its bafis in a party diftinction, and is determinable only by party principles. The refolution for fufpending the execution of the Company's orders on the

20th

20th July, 1778, was notified to the Court of Directors in our difpatches by the Eagle packet, dated the 17th Auguft. Their anfwer may be received, and ought to be expected, before the period which the Act of Parliament has prefcribed for the duration of this government. To prevent their orders, by an intermediate decifion of a point of fuch magnitude referred to them, is neither, in my judgment, confiftent with the refpect which is due to their authority, nor with the actual ftate of this government, already oppreffed with difficulties which demand the ftrenuous and united exertion of all its powers, and which it tends to throw into utter confufion; and for what! Let the perfon who made the motion fay, what is the object of it. Is the reinftatement, as it is called, of Mr. Francis Fowke to an office which he never held, of fuch weighty confequence to the interefts of the Eaft India Company, and of the Britifh nation in India, that for this the firft executive member of their firft government muft be treated with infult, and either keep his feat, to be a partaker of a fcene of anarchy and confufion during the fhort but momentous interval which remains of the power which we unitedly hold, or leave it and a government embarraffed with new and perhaps greater diftractions?

I defire that the paragraphs of the general letter and the extract of our proceedings, which have been read, may be entered after the firft motion made by Mr. Francis. I moft earneftly recommend them to the ferious attention and reflection of the other members of this board, and to thofe of the Commander in Chief moft efpecially. I hope that the decifion on this queftion will not be precipitated; that the confequences of it may be weighed, before an act fo critical and decifive be irrevocably paffed. I came unprepared for it, not ignorant, indeed, that it would be brought on at an early time, for the public voice has loudly announced it; but I did not expect to be furprized with it on a day, and in a department, devoted to bufinefs, from which this is entirely foreign. I therefore hope and requeft that the other members will fufpend their decifion until the next meeting of the board in the general department.

Mr.

Mr. Francis. The prefent queftion does not properly lie between the Governor General and me, but between this board and that authority which the legiflature has placed over us. The propriety of waiting for farther orders, when we have pofitive orders before us, may at any time be pleaded with equal reafon as at prefent and may as eafily defeat any future orders, however peremptory, in confirmation of the paft, as thofe which we have already received. The perfonal appeal made to Sir Eyre Coote obliges me to take this opportunity of affuring him, that I will never bring any queftion of this nature forward, in which it will be poffible for a member of this board to take part againft me, without at the fame time taking part againft the Court of Directors. As for the reft, I fhall content myfelf with faying, that the Governor General has formed a very erroneous judgment of my intentions.

If the public voice has already announced my defign to introduce the prefent motion, it is a ftrong prefumptive proof of the public expectation and, as I think, of of their judgment upon the refolution which I propofe to have reverfed. As for myfelf, I declare upon my honour, and if there be that man living who can contradict me let him come forward, that I never did directly or indirectly, or by the moft diftant intimation, acquaint any perfon, not a member of this board, of my defign to move the prefent queftion. As the Governor General expected it and as the queftion itfelf is of a very plain and fimple nature, I think there is no ground for deferring the decifion of it. At all events, I have done my duty and fhall give the board no further trouble.

Sir Eyre Coote. Being called upon by my King and country to fill a poft in this part of the world of the higheft importance to the ftate, it was with the greateft diffidence I undertook that fervice, well knowing the great difficulties I had to encounter from the unfortunate differences which had arifen among the members of the Supreme Council. I therefore determined not to take a part in thofe differences, it being, in my opinion,

D   the

the fureft method that I could devife of putting an end
to them; and conceiving that any kind of retrofpeft
would prove fatal to my wifhes, was determined to prevent them as much as lay in my power, by bringing forward no matter, the decifion of which I was not immediately anfwerable for the confequences of; paying at
the fame time implicit obedience to the orders of the
Court of Directors, which I am determined to adhere to
for my line of conduct. I agree to fufpend the decifion
of the queftion till the next meeting of the Council in
the general department.

Mr. Wheler. It cannot be confidered precipitate in
me to give an immediate opinion upon the prefent
queftion, my fentiments being already recorded. I
therefore, to prevent the implication of giving a hafty
opinion, defire leave to record my further fentiments at
this meeting of the board.

Mr. Barwell. I feel much concerned on the prefent
occafion. The forcing on a queftion on a matter that
has paffed judgment, and which, if decided, muft be a
confirmation or reverfion of that judgment, independent
of the authority to which it is fubmitted, will, I fear, not
tend to conciliate the differences of the board, which I
flattered myfelf might have drawn to a period. The
confequences are very obvious. I hope, however, the
temper and moderation of Sir Eyre Coote will decide
for terminating the diftractions which have hitherto prevailed. It is with great pleafure I obferve in the de-
livery of Sir Eyre's fentiments a refolution, fo decidedly
expreffed, of confulting alone the honour and interefts
of the government and fixing our councils, if poffible, to
that particular point only. I am fo well aware of the
confequences to refult from haftily deciding on an act of
the adminiftration, under the prefent change in its cir-
cumftances in the arrival of Sir Eyre Coote, that I entirely concur in the wifh expreffed by the Governor
General to fufpend the queftion.

Mr. Wheler. As the members of the board have not
objected to my requeft of entering my opinion upon the

main

main queftion, I beg leave to do it in the following words ; That, as I cannot difcover, either in the minute entered by the Governor General, or in the 25th paragraph of our general letter to the Court of Directors of the 17th Auguft by the Eagle packet, the fhadow of an argument that can induce me to alter my former opinion, much lefs juftify me in the difobedience of a pofitive order from the Court of Directors, I am for the queftion.

Refolved, that the decifion of the queftion propofed by Mr. Francis be fufpended until the next meeting of the board in this department.

No. XVI.

Extract of Bengal Public Confultations, the 5th April, 1779. Prefent, the Governor General, Meffrs. Barwell, Francis, and Wheler, and Sir Eyre Coote.

MR Francis's motion, recorded in the laft confultation, being now again taken into confideration, Lieutenant-General Sir Eyre Coote delivers in the following minute.

Since the laft meeting of the board in this department, I have had time to reflect very maturely upon the nature and tendency of the queftion now depending.

In my former minute upon the fubject, I declared the two ruling principles of my conduct to be, the defire of avoiding every kind of retrofpect, and a firm refolution to pay an implicit obedience to the orders of the Company.

And however difficult it may feem to reconcile an adherence to both under the prefent circumftance, fince, by paffing an opinion on the queftion I fhould feem to fwerve from the one, and by declining it to lofe fight of the other, I yet flatter myfelf that the conduct which agrees with my own feelings will alfo meet with the approbation of this board.

D 2   I declare

I declare therefore, that had I had the honour of a feat here at the time the Company's inſtructions reſpecting Mr. Fowke were received, I ſhould certainly have joined moſt heartily with thoſe gentlemen who were for putting them into immediate execution, as I ſhall ever do in regard to any future orders which may be given by the Company while I remain in the ſervice. But as the whole of this tranſaction paſſed before my arrival, and as the reſult of the laſt proceedings thereupon now lies before the Directors for their ultimate deciſion, I deſire to wave the giving any preſent opinion upon it and to reſerve my vote till their orders are received, when I ſhall moſt aſſuredly give it in ſupport of them.

Mr. Francis. The queſtion is, whether a poſitive order of the Court of Directors ſhall or ſhall not be obeyed. I ſuppoſe it is hardly neceſſary for me to ſay what my opinion is: I act in conformity to it in giving my vote for the queſtion.

Mr. Barwell. Mr. Francis muſt excuſe me if I cannot receive the queſtion as it ſtands explained by him: I apprehend no one who ſhall take the whole ſubject into his conſideration will allow it to be ſo compendious. It is not a queſtion on the Company's orders. However, I am willing to ſuppreſs the reflections that ariſe in my mind to the harmony of our future councils. I am againſt the queſtion.

The Governor General. It is unneceſſary to expreſs my further ſenſe of the queſtion, or the manner in which it has been concluded; I ſhall therefore only ſay that I am againſt the queſtion.

Mr. Francis's queſtion reſolved in the negative.

Mr. Francis. I beg leave to enter my diſſent and proteſt againſt the reſolution.

No. XVII.

Extract of the General Letter from Bengal, dated the 22d April 1779.]

Par. 12. A Motion was made at one of our meetings, that the orders contained in the 65th, 66th, and 67th paragraphs of your general letter of the 30th January 1778, should be carried into execution : The question was resolved in the negative; and we beg leave to refer you to our proceedings on this subject for your more particular information.

No. XVIII.

Extract of the Company's General Letter to Bengal, dated 14th May, 1779.

Par. 4. IN answer to the 25th paragraph of your letter of the 17th August last, respecting the appointment we assigned to Mr. Francis Fowke, we only remark, that as the consultations are not yet before us, we must defer our decision on the subject and hope the reasons which swayed you, so far as to induce you to suspend the execution of a positive and peremptory order of the Court of Directors, will be found sufficient to justify your conduct on that extraordinary occasion.

No. XIX.

Extract of the Company's General Letter to Bengal, dated 27th May, 1779.

Par. 40. WE have read with astonishment your formal resolution to suspend the execution of our orders relative to Mr. Francis Fowke; your proceedings at large are now before us; we shall take such
measures

meafures as appear neceffary for preferving the authority of the Court of Directors and for preventing fuch
inftances of direct and wilful difobedience in our fer-
vants in time to come. At prefent we repeat the commands contained in the 67th paragraph of our letter of
the 30th of January 1778, and direct that they be carried into immediate execution.

No. XX.

*Extract of Bengal Public Confultations, the 27th Fe-
bruary 1780. Prefent, the Governor General, and
Meffrs. Francis and Wheler. Mr. Barwell indifpofed.*

READ the 40th paragraph of the general letter
from the Hon. the Court of Directors, dated 27th
May 1779.
Agreed, that Mr. Francis Fowke be appointed Refident at Benares, in conformity to the intention of the
Court of Directors; and that Mr. Thomas Graham be
directed to deliver over the charge of that office to him
on his arrival there.

No. XXI.

*Extract of the General Letter from Bengal, dated 3d
March, 1780.*

Par. 46. WE have the honour to acquaint you, that
in conformity to your laft commands of
the 27th May 1779, Mr. Francis Fowke has been
appointed Refident at Benares, and Mr. Thomas Graham
recalled from the ftation.

No.

No. XXII.

Copy of an Addrefs to the Court of Directors from Lieutenant Colonel John Walfh.

To the Hon. the Court of Directors of the United Eaft India Company.

Honourable,

Eaft India Houfe, 2d January 1782.

I Yefterday received a letter from Calcutta, informing me that my nephew Francis Fowke was, on the 12th January 1781, again difmiffed from his office at Benares, to which he had, not quite a twelvemonth before, returned in confequence of your own exprefs orders, but which were not permitted to take place till reiterated in the ftrongeft terms; that his affiftant Mr. Markham, certainly a moft unexceptionable young gentleman and I believe by no one more efteemed than by my nephew, was nominated in his room; and that the reverfion of the Agency for fupplying the army with boats was intended for him, but as this agency could not take place till the September following, he would be permitted to draw for his ufual falary at Benares of 1000 rupees a month to that time and three months after. Left the favourable terms in which, as I underftand, he is mentioned in the very minutes, by which he is removed from Benares, fhould induce your Honors to fuppofe that he had acquiefced in the meafure, I have to affure you from his neareft relations in Calcutta, to whofe knowledge it had come, that they confider it as a fevere injury and a great misfortune. I am informed that the public advices from Bengal do not reach to the time of this tranfaction, but I muft neverthelefs entreat, as I can produce indubitable proofs of its exiftence, that the prefent difpatch to India may convey redrefs to a

Servant,

Servant, I will prefume to fay of Merit, deprived of the office which you yourfelves exprefsly and repeatedly have confirmed to him.

I have the honour to be with Refpect,

Honourable,

Your moft obedient,

and moft humble fervant,

JOHN WALSH.

No. XXIII.

Extract of a Letter from the Governor General and Council to the Court of Directors, dated 3d February 1781, received 4th January 1782.

MR. Francis Fowke recalled from Benares and appointed Agent for the provifion of boats to the army after the expiration of the prefent contract. Mr. Markham appointed Refident at Benares.

No. XXIV.

Copy of an Addrefs to the Court of Directors from Lieutenant Colonel John Walfh.

To the Hon. the Court of Directors of the United Eaft India Company.

Chefterfield-ftreet, 23d January 1782.

Honourable,

AS the public advices to Bengal by the fhips now under difpatch are on the point of being clofed, I humbly requeft to know if my letter of the 2d inftant, concerning the Recal of my nephew Francis Fowke from Benares, has been taken into confideration; and

whether

whether any and what redrefs your Honours have been pleafed to order by this difpatch to be made to him, on account of his removal from an office, to which he was appointed by exprefs orders from the Court of Directors, dated 30th January 1778; the execution, however, of which the government of Bengal thought proper to fufpend, on different pleas at different times, yet none impeaching the merit of Mr. Francis Fowke, until the arrival of reiterated commands from you, dated 27th May 1779, when he was permitted to proceed to Benares, according to your appointment. This was fomething more than a year and a half after the receipt of your firft orders for his immediate re-inftatement as Refident there, and more than three years after his firft Recal from thence; all which time he was detained in Calcutta without employ, without appointments, without any recompence, not even the falary of his office made good to him. Whatever hope may be entertained of exacter obedience to the orders which you may be induced to give on this occafion to the government of Bengal, I cannot avoid, as guardian to the juft rights of my nephew, requefting the interference of the Court of Directors in like manner as it was formerly granted by them, when the injuftice of his firft removal from Benares appeared manifeft to them. A public letter from the goverment of Bengal, dated 3d February 1781, lately received, contains official information of his frefh Recal from Benares, and nomination to be Agent for the provifion of boats to the army after the expiration of the prefent contract; alfo of Mr. Markham's appointment to be the Refident in his room. If it is not evident on the face of this meafure that it is arbitrary, in violation of your own appointment, and of ferious detriment to both the character and fortune of Mr. Francis Fowke; if it is not evident that he could not have confented to be deprived of a public honourable charge appointed by yourfelves, for the promife of a private, obfcure, and precarious office, unattended even with the lure of pecuniary advantage, the moft convincing documents to demonftrate it may be produced; but as Major John

E   Scott,

Scott, lately arrived from Bengal, and acting here in behalf of the Governor General in his private concerns, did both converse and correspond with Mr. Francis Fowke on this subject, he can, and I doubt not but he readily will, satisfy your honourable Court, that these measures were taken without the consent of Mr. Francis Fowke. It is equally evident, that public necessity was not the ground for the removal of Mr. Francis Fowke, for what public benefit could arise from displacing a senior servant, promoted to the office for his knowledge in the Persian tongue and unexceptionable good character, and remarked by the Court of Directors to have executed it with the greatest punctuality and exactness, and putting in his room a junior servant, of whose age, time of service, experience in the affairs of Benares, and knowledge of the Oriental languages, you cannot but be well informed. Even the wretched plea of party necessity could not be urged at the time for the measure; for it is well known that when it took place, two parties did not exist in Bengal.

On these considerations your honourable Court cannot but see pressing reasons for giving substantial and early redress to an aggrieved servant, suffering in contempt of your own orders.

I have the honour to be with Respect,
Honourable,
Your most obedient,
and most humble servant,
JOHN WALSH.

No. XXV.

Copy of a Letter from the Secretary of the Court of Directors to Lieutenant Colonel John Walsh.

Sir,

I AM ordered by the Court of Directors of the East India Company to acquaint you that the two letters you addressed the Court, dated the 2d and 23d instant,
are

are referred to the Committee of Correfpondence, and that the faid Committee have not yet come to any determination thereon.

I am, Sir,

Eaft India Houfe, 29th January 1782.

Your obedient humble fervant,

P. M I C H E L L, Sec:

Lieut. Colonel John Walfh.

No. XXVI.

Extract of the Secret General Letter from Bengal, dated 27th April 1781, received by the Bellmont, 5th February 1782.

Par. 46. MR. Francis Fowke having been recalled from his refidency at Benares, and appointed Agent for the provifion of boats to the army after the expiration of the prefent contract, We have appointed Mr. William Markham to that Refidency.

No. XXVII.

Extract from Bengal Secret Confultations, furnifhed by favour of Major John Scott, the original Records not having hitherto reached the India Houfe.

Confultation, 14th January 1781.

GOVERNOR General. While this government is charged with fuch extenfive concerns, and hath to contend with difficluties equal perhaps to thofe in which even the fupreme adminiftration of the Britifh empire is at this moment involved, it may at leaft claim as a right which, under any other fyftem of government

E 2   that

that hath ever yet exifted, would be conferred on it as
an indifpenfable obligation,. to employ and exercife the
powers which are inherent in its conftitution, and which
are immediately neceffary to the fupport, and eventually
to the exiftence, of thofe effential interefts which it holds
in charge. On this principle I claim the right of nomi-
nating the Agent of my own choice to the Refidency of
Benares: it is a reprefentative ftation and cannot, without a contradiction, be the charge of a man not prefe-
rably chofen to it by the members of the actual government, and holding it by an authority independent of
of theirs. Speaking for myfelf alone, it may be fufficient
to affirm that Mr. Francis Fowke is not my agent; that
I cannot give him my confidence; that while he conti-
nues at Benares he ftands as a fcreen between the Raja
and this government, inftead of an inftrument of con-
troul; and that the Raja himfelf, and every chief in In-
doftan, will regard it as the pledge and foundation of his
independence.

To Mr. Fowke himfelf I have no perfonal objection.
I approve his conduct and efteem his character; and I
believe I might depend upon his exact and literal obedience and fidelity in the execution of the functions annexed to it. My objection is ftated above, and it is in-
fuperable.

The perfon whom I have chofen to fucceed him I confider as ftanding in the fame degree of confidence and
eftimation with Mr. Wheler as myfelf. I adopted him
(if I may fo exprefs myfelf) from his family and patronage, and affigned him an office of the higheft truft
near my own perfon with Mr. Wheler's approbation;
and from a forefight of the event which has fince made
us the copartners of this government, and which fug-
gefted to me the propriety of employing fuch Agents as
would be agreeable to him while they poffeffed the other
requifites for my own confidence,

I therefore think him on every confideration the fitteft
to fill the office in queftion. I therefore move that Mr.
Francis Fowke be immediately removed from the Refidency of Benares, and that Mr. Markham may be appointed to it in his ftead,

While

While I thus acquit myfelf of what I conceive to be a a public duty, it is my defire at the fame time to indemnify Mr. Fowke from the confequences perfonally attending it towards him. I therefore move that he be at the fame time invefted with the appointment of Agent for all boats to be employed for the military fervice of this eftablifhment, with an allowance of a commiffion of 15 per cent. upon all his difburfements in this office; that the executive charge thereof take place from the period of the expiration of Colonel Morgan's prefent contract, and that till that time and for three months following it, he be allowed to draw his prefent allowance of 1000 Rupees per month.

I propofe this method in preference to a contract, becaufe I am convinced from experience that the fervice will be better performed by this alteration, although it is liable to one material objection in its natural influence in his expences. This is a defect which can only be corrected by the probity of the perfon who is intrufted with fo important a charge; and I am willing to have it underftood as a proof of the confidence which I repofe in Mr. Fowke, that I have propofed his appointment, in oppofition to a general principle, to a truft fo conftituted.

Mr. Wheler. I accede to the propriety of the Governor General's arguments, and think them particularly applicable to the prefent ftate of this government. I am alfo highly flattered by the choice the Governor General has made of a Gentleman to fill this important ftation, who was formerly under my patronage, and who is ftill in my confidence. But as Mr. Fowke has not yet fignified his willingnefs to accept of the compenfation propofed to him in exchange for his prefent appointment, I muft decline giving my affent to his immediate removal.

The Governor General's motion being agreed to, Refolved, that Mr. William Markham be accordingly appointed Refident at Benares, and Mr. Benn his affiftant. Refolved, that Mr. Francis Fowke be invefted with the appointment of Agent for the provifion of all boats to be employed for the military fervices of this eftablifh-

ment,

ment, with an allowance of a commiffion of 1·5 per cent. upon all his difburfements in this office, the executive charge of which is to take place from the period of the expiration of Colonel Morgan's contract, and that to that time, and for three months following it, he be permitted to draw the prefent allowance of 1000 Rupees per month.